Upside Down is a great resource for adoptive parents and the ones who love them, wisely and compassionately shining a light on the deep challenges involved in parenting children with wounded hearts. If you are such a parent, this book will help you feel supported and understood. If you know and love such a family, you will come away from this book with a whole new level of understanding, and be better able to support your loved ones.

—Mary Ostyn, author of *Forever Mom:*
What to Expect When You're Adopting

Shannon writes with raw, real, and hopeful narrative. We would recommend this book to any adoptive family facing attachment issues with their child, and to those who desire to understand and support them.

—Mike and Kristin Berry, founders of
Confessions of an Adoptive Parent
www.confessionsofanadoptiveparent.com

Shannon Guerra's book, *Upside Down*, will at once resonate with the adoptive family, and educate their loved ones. This gem of a book is a manual that reads like a letter from a dear old friend. The "nuts and bolts" of living in an attachment-challenged home have never been as warmly and succinctly addressed as in Shannon's book. Her words are a balm to the weary soul, and should be required reading for anyone who is considering adoption, has adopted, or knows an adoptive family. Beyond that, every counselor, pediatrician, psychologist, and attachment specialist should have this on hand as a resource for themselves and their clients. Yes, it's that good.

—Cynthia Hellman, adoptive mama

Upside Down is a trip to the refreshing well of empathetic understanding for parents of attachment-challenged children. Shannon Guerra's book, from cover to cover, delivers a safe haven that comes from experience. Getting away with fellow foster and adoptive parents

for a weekend retreat is often not possible. Thankfully, we have the next best option in our hands with this very book.

—Debi Rice, foster and adoptive mama

Shannon Guerra offers a light-hearted, easy read to address a difficult subject. Traumatic experiences can seriously affect early relationships and bonding for children. In *Upside Down*, we are offered insight from a mother who wrestles with these challenges daily. If you are fostering or adopting a child, read this book. You will gain insight into the mind of a child who doesn't trust love. If you are a parent, grandparent, friend, minister, dentist, or doctor, read this book. Learn to care for the heart of a child by caring for the heart of the parent. *Upside Down* helps us to care without judgment, while developing the counter-intuitive behaviors we must acquire to support families as they bond.

—Julia Bolles, Special Needs Ministry Lead at
Church on the Rock
Wasilla, AK

As an adoptive momma to five kiddos, all from super hard places, I appreciated this book and every single word written in it. This book was all the words I needed and wanted to say but written so much better than I could have ever said it myself. I live this book daily. I read *Upside Down* in one sitting, then again the next day. So powerful, simple, and spoken with such truth. Thank you for writing this powerful book.

—Nicole M., mom of nine children

Sharing from her wealth of knowledge on the subject of attachment in adoption and from her family's own experience with it, Shannon has written a wonderful book that really helps people understand what adoptive parents may be going through on a day-to-day basis with their adopted children and how one can best support them in their journey of attachment. Encouraging, honest, and engaging - this book should be on every person's shelf who is/has adopted or has someone who is adopted in their life.

—Britney Carr, pastor's wife and missionary in Asia

Upside Down, Understanding and Supporting Attachment in Adoptive Families by Shannon Guerra is an amazing resource of help to those who have friends and family who have adopted. The approach is both funny and sobering at the same time. It gives a glimpse into the trials parents of adopted children face, gives suggestions on boundaries, and shares real stories and insights from parents in the adoptive trenches. It is a must read for every friend and family member of adoptive families. You will learn a lot…and learn you have much to learn. I had no idea of the effects of RAD (Reactive Attachment Disorder). I am humbled to read this book. I will recommend this book. I will reread this book many times. Read it for yourself and begin the journey of understanding and the support that is deeply needed.

—Ed Waken, pastor of ValleyLife Church

Over five years ago Jesus led our family of three to join our hearts with God's heart through the journey of foster care and ultimately adoption. Now, three infant girls later, our "forever family" of six is in the thick of our new journey with both its joys and its challenges.

As a pastor of a large church and a father of four *(plus a german shorthair)*, it isn't very often that I come across someone who so clearly "gets us." Yet, Shannon has captured the life of an adoptive family in a way that brought me to tears time and again as I read the words from her heart on the pages of her book.

If you want to understand and support adoptive families or if you just want to know someone is "in it with you" as an adoptive family, Shannon's book is a must read!

—Jonathan Walker, lead pastor at Church on the Rock
Wasilla, AK

upside down

down

understanding and
supporting attachment
in adoptive families

shannon guerra

WESTBOW
PRESS®
A DIVISION OF THOMAS NELSON
& ZONDERVAN

Scripture quotations are from The Holy Bible, English Standard Version® (ESV®), copyright © 2001 by Crossway, a publishing ministry of Good News Publishers. Used by permission. All rights reserved.

WestBow Press books may be ordered through booksellers or by contacting:

WestBow Press
A Division of Thomas Nelson & Zondervan
1663 Liberty Drive
Bloomington, IN 47403
www.westbowpress.com
1 (866) 928-1240

ISBN: 978-1-5127-5962-4 (sc)
ISBN: 978-1-5127-5963-1 (e)

Print information available on the last page.

WestBow Press rev. date: 1/16/2017

to Cody and Sara,
who have long been our heroes

and

to Larry and Sharon,
who have loved us well

contents

introduction

Our family is not glamorous. We are loud and messy, quiet and nerdy, transparent and complicated. We were all of those things before adoption, and now we are just...more so.

There are eight of us: two parents and six kids (four biological, two adopted), plus three cats, living in a three-bedroom house in Alaska. Some days are hard and plodding, some days are surprisingly easy, but in either case, bedtime usually feels like the finish line after a twelve-hour sprint.

Our kiddos – most of them – love to be carried upside down to bed. There's squealing, shrieking, and giggling when my husband grabs one of them by the legs and swings them upside down, hauling them up the stairs to be flung into their beds. Alas, he doesn't do this with our 13-year-old anymore.

One night after many hard months, our son Andrey had pushed us away all day – he does it, mostly, by pushing himself away from us – and Vince picked him up before bedtime. Held him by the stairs. Hugged him, smiled at him. Got a little smile out of him, too. Bounced him a little, for the beginnings of a giggle. And then...he started to swing him upside down.

Andrey screamed bloody murder, terrified.

Vince picked him up again and held him. Andrey did not trust that he would not drop him on his head, and I suspect he had the glimmer of a guilty conscience that recognized his behavior might have made it somewhat tempting to do so.

This trust issue is a biggie, and we've gotten past several small things with our adopted children, Andrey and Reagan: high-fives don't result in terrified screams anymore, Duck-Duck-Goose is tolerable, and ecstatic shouts of "slug bug white!" followed by friendly jabs no longer initiate cowering and tears.

They still don't wrestle with Daddy and the other kids, though. The grey area between rough-housing and violence is too shady for them to know they're safe.

After two years in our family, they still need convincing about safety, love, and trust. They start to believe it sometimes but get scared and push us away. They've known rejection and abandonment, and they test with every broken tool they've gathered to see if we will reject and abandon them, too.

Will you really care for me? Even when I push you away? Even if I repulse you, are you really for real? If I persist in self-destruct mode, will you really stay, for good, forever?

No one has before. You can't really love me. Surely.

But we do.

They have great value. They need to believe it, though.

They've been home for two years, but they were in institutions for more than eighty months. In those first, most formative three years, Andrey was in an institution that has become infamous,[1] and somehow lived through it. His behavior tells the story for him.[2]

Often, he or Reagan – or both at the same time, which is *so awesome*, almost like having a double root canal without anesthesia – still refuse to participate in basic family routines. They don't trust them, they want to be in control. And sometimes they're dealing with fallout from interacting with other adults, which is confusing for them because they've never known family or forever before – and they're still in the process of being convinced that we are their family, forever. We limit their interaction with other adults as much as possible to help the convincing. It feels upside down for all of us.

We all need convincing at some point. The Creator of the world turned everything upside down to show us we were valuable, cared for, and loved – His own children, for good, forever – and the Savior let Himself be shattered to save the broken.

Whoever would save his life will lose it, but whoever loses his life for My sake will find it.

For what will it profit a man if he gains the whole world and forfeits his soul?

—Matthew 16:25-26a

For some of us, it takes a long time to believe it. We don't trust Him, we want to be in control, and we're confused.

Will you really care for me? Even when I push you away? Even if I repulse you, are you really for real? If I persist in self-destruct mode, will you really stay for good, forever?

No one has before. You can't really love me. Surely.

But He does.

He's teaching us how to love like He does, and it's the most refining, sanctifying process I've ever experienced.

This book is for adoptive families who need to know that **you are not alone** in what often feels like a very lonely journey in this upside-down life. I share it with you not as an expert, but as an adoptive mama in the trenches and learning alongside you, with the help of dozens of other adoptive families who have been kind enough to contribute their own experiences. Collectively we span the entire spectrum ranging from general attachment issues to Reactive Attachment Disorder (RAD).

This book is also for family, friends, churches, and community members. It is crucial for these groups to understand the mission field of adoptive families in the trenches so they can walk beside them in a more supportive way.

Included are several ideas for communicating about these oh-so-special needs with others. There are links with resources, and input from both professionals and long-time adoptive parents.

I hope you'll find comforting camaraderie, and only as much sarcasm as is absolutely necessary. This information is not intended to diagnose, treat, cure, or prevent any disease. That is what chocolate is for.

one

the reality behind the rose-tinted movies

She has a son around six years old. His pictures are on the wall near the sink and the dental equipment. She tells me a little about him – school, video games, toys.

"I hear you have a lot of kids," she says. Friendly, casual.

"Yep, six."

And then the conversation takes a sudden turn downhill.

"How many of them are your real kids?"

Exhale slowly, smile. "They're all my real kids."

I can see she senses she's made a blunder. She tries to correct, or clarify, or something. "I mean, how many of them do you *really* have? Only some of them are actually *yours,* right?"

SHANNON GUERRA

The misstep is over-corrected by an italicized do-si-do and lands both feet firmly in her mouth.

"I *really* have six kids," I answer. "Two of them were adopted, but they're all mine…and they're all real." *Smile, mama.* No wonder the dentist mentioned I clench my teeth.

Even before our adoption was complete, we realized there are a lot of false notions about adoption and adoptive families. We were guilty of many of them before we entered the process, too.

The rest of the appointment goes well and the staff works hard to respect boundaries with our daughter. As we leave, the assistant tells me that Reagan did wonderfully.

I don't have time to teach her Attachment and Adoption 101. But since we'll be back here again often, I want her to understand a little bit about our family and why those peculiar boundaries are in place.

I tell her that it's not so much how Reagan behaved during the appointment, but how she behaves over the next day or so that really determines how it went. Like many kids healing from attachment issues, she usually doesn't act out her anxiety in front of strangers; she saves behavioral fallout for her family instead. The colors of any bruising caused by too much attention, stimuli, or interaction won't show up until we're home.

"Oh, I know," the assistant nods. "Yep, I have a kid, too."

*Sure. Mm-hmm...**you have no idea**.* I gave up trying to explain. I smiled and nodded, and by some miracle I didn't even feel an urge to use the sharp, pointy dental tools conveniently nearby in a violent manner.

It's hard on both sides, and it can be terribly awkward sometimes. People want to be warm and fuzzy to the children. I get that, but it's not therapeutic for the child and it's often devastating to the family. Sometimes people pretend to understand; sometimes they assume they do. And other times when we try to help them understand, people take obvious offense when we set boundaries that seem unusual.

> *For a while, people still see them as poor orphans and want to love on them. They need to see that these are **your** children and not poor orphans anymore... Lay down the law. Stop asking nicely. If this was your biological kid, they would already respect that. At least that has been my experience.*
>
> *—adoptive mother*

One of the hardest things for our own family is trying to protect Andrey and Reagan in public from seemingly normal interactions with others. So much of their negative behavior at home is triggered by the well-meaning but devastatingly misplaced kindness and sympathy of others.

It is difficult for friends and family who haven't dealt with attachment issues to understand why we are so weird about things like that. I think sometimes people refuse to understand because they want your children to be "their" niece/nephew, or "their" grandchild, etc. And while that's important, they don't get that these kids haven't been anybody's anything for so long that they need to get this first, most important, relationship (with Mom and Dad) right first.

—adoptive mother

For a child struggling with attachment, attention from other adults is often like giving sugar to a diabetic child whose body cannot process it correctly. It is confusing, misleading, and damaging to them. Affectionate interaction from other adults is poisonous, but when it comes from their parents it is their medicine. If other adults give them attention though, it often prevents them from taking the medicine from their parents.

Many people have asked us, "Why have we never heard of this?" We've asked that, too.

After some time to think about it, I came up with a few reasons:

Anne of Green Gables. Oliver Twist. Rose-tinted made-for-TV movies and other media about adoption.

I love Anne. And I love Charles Dickens. But the books are always better than the movies, and unfortunately people imagine adoption to be like the movie version, Disney-fied.

A few months ago I watched a beautifully idyllic short video on adoption about a childless couple who struggled with infertility for years, and they finally adopted a beautiful baby straight from the hospital. It seemed so perfect, and although it was a hard road for that family to get there, the video didn't show the struggle. And the family still has challenges ahead, but the video didn't allude to any of that, either.

The baby drinks formula because his adoptive mama who loves him and holds him in this short film is not the one who gave birth to him. As I watch, I remember Andrey and Reagan must have had some version of formula, too. They were never nursed by a mama, and they missed that physical and emotional nourishment.

The couple and their baby leave the hospital, and I think, *What about his biological mom?* I wonder if the nurse who handed the baby to the new parents is the same nurse who just helped deliver the baby from his biological mother. If she is, she has seen the full whiplash of heartache on one side and joy on the other.

After watching the video, I thought about my son Andrey who was starved and hungry for years, but that very night he had refused dinner because of attachment issues he's struggling through as a result of his traumatic past. I want him filled and growing in every way, but nourishment for him and Reagan looks so different. It's not romantic – it's gritty, messy, painful, and disappointing. We want beauty, bonding, and nurturing peace with them, but they fight this daily[1] – they fight us, they fight themselves, they fight their past. We fight for their future.

Attachment issues might be unheard of because most people have never been through the process of completing a home study in order to qualify to care for children who have endured abandonment, grief, and trauma. Attachment issues are often considered the most difficult disability to live with. Part of that is simply because what people see on the outside is not the reality in the home, and the parents feel like people won't believe them if they talk about it. Or that others will judge them if they do talk about it. Or that they will make adoption look bad, their own parenting look bad, or their child look bad.

There's a lot of fear to deal with. The children fight their own fears, and the parents fight an entirely different set of fears. Our relationships change. Our lifestyle and social lives change. Our involvement in the community changes.

Everything turns upside down, and it is incredibly difficult to know how honest and transparent we should be about it.

We want to be truthful. But we also want to protect our children, their story, and our family as a whole. We want to protect and encourage the adoption process.

We have no idea how to merge all of those realities.

And we all do it differently. Some people share a lot, some don't share anything. In our own family, in our blog, in about three posts a month, I share less than five percent of what goes on in our home. There's just too much; it's too raw, too repetitive, and too personal to give any more information.

Also, *attachment* as a special need is a relatively new concept in the realm of adoption and foster care. Most families who dealt with these issues ten years ago had no term for it.

Even in more recent years, it's possible to know nothing about attachment issues if a person doesn't intimately know any adoptive or foster families. Or maybe they do know these families, and their experiences have been perfect, ideal, and rose-colored. I'm sure it happens. They might be perfect parents with perfect children.

Or maybe, life has been very un-perfect and the parents have dealt with this quietly, and cried behind closed doors, knowing that most people don't understand and many won't even bother to try. Maybe they think they are alone. Maybe they *are* alone, and desperately in need of support and prayer.

Maybe they are pioneers, bravely, persistently, and painfully plowing the trail that others – including us – have tried to follow. It's easier for us because of them. Some of the dirt and snow has blown over the path and we still have to dig, but we can see where their tracks went, where they had to double-back, and where they found a truer course.

They have made the way much easier for us, enabling us to be a little more vocal about our own experience while they had to learn in painful silence. We share our experiences with others, praying they will find understanding, safety, and hope.

Because this is no Disney movie, friends. *This is our story.* And it's not finished yet.

two

the why behind the weird limits

Other than all of the times I've walked into the protruding foot of a coffee table and smashed my toes so hard that I saw lights sparkle, I've never broken a bone or worn a hard cast. So, unless broken toes count (and I don't think they do, even though my husband claims he heard me swear in tongues once when I walked into a bench…but he could be exaggerating) I really have no idea what I'm talking about.

But as far as my primitive knowledge goes, a broken bone – as long as it's not a toe – is usually covered with a cast in order to protect it from further harm while it heals. No one touches the bone after it is set and covered with the cast, and the bone has all the time it needs to regrow. It has the safe environment it needs to keep from hurting itself or grating the tissue around it. But people *can* touch the cast – in fact, they are encouraged to. They sign it, draw on it, and show their love for the broken person by attending to the cast.

Like that broken bone, the broken child is set into their family for healing and protection. Parents of children with attachment issues are the cast that protects them while they heal. They are firmly wrapped around these children as a sturdy wall that will take all the beatings necessary to keep the broken ones inside safe while they regrow. It is crucial that no one touches the child until it is safe to do so, both for the child's sake and the sake of those surrounding the child – their sharp edges must be treated with care.

> *We ask that you let Mom do the nurturing and heart healing rather than step in and fill him up so he can push Mom's love away longer. They say "the best way to show love to a child is by loving their mom." The professionals tell us that RAD family members need seven hugs a day to facilitate healing – feel free to offer your healing hugs to Mom anytime!*
>
> —*Nancy Thomas*[1]

The best way to show love and support for the child is to love the cast – their parents. Hug them, encourage them, tell them they are doing an amazing job. Don't touch or expose the broken bone, though, until they say it's okay.

There are many different special needs that aren't visibly obvious – some medical, some not – and attachment is one of them.

It takes emotional effort to explain these needs and boundaries. Adoptive parents know it sounds weird; we live this weirdness out daily. It is frustrating and sad for us as parents to have to ask other adults not to interact with our children. It's especially painful for us (and our children) to have to explain this to people *in front of them,* though sometimes it must be done. We try to do it lightly if our kids are right there, but sometimes that backfires and people misunderstand the seriousness of the issue.

So, since it can't be seen, let me illustrate:

Imagine a pendulum, settled in the middle. This pendulum is our child, and we are standing right with them at the center place of rest and equilibrium.

One catch, though – attachment issues are a special need. For our situation, that means this particular pendulum is magnetically charged, and so are we. And so are other adults.

And here we are, standing with our little child, attaching. Bonding, sticking together as magnets do.

Another adult comes near and an interesting thing happens. The presence of this adult – even an adult who respects boundaries, understands the situation, and kindly ignores our attachment-challenged children – creates a little pull on the pendulum. It's no biggie, though, because this adult knows what's happening and does not dote on, speak to, or otherwise engage our child. This marvelously helpful person does not respond to our child's staring, movement, and other attempts to make eye contact or attract attention.

We have our conversation and the adult leaves. Our child settles right back with us, with minimal to no swinging afterward. It's weird, yes, but it works.

Something far more interesting happens when an adult who does not understand or respect their special needs comes near. They approach and the little magnetic pull is still there, but this person immediately flashes a glowing smile at our child, or they ruffle his hair, saying, "Oh, he's so cute!" or, "What a doll!"

These are totally normal, sweet, acceptable interactions to have with most kids. We have four kiddos that won't bat an eye at this and they'll be fine afterward. We gave birth to them, they had a healthy beginning, they are attached to us. They aren't magnetic and they won't swing.

But our children with attachment issues feel a very strong tug for every response. They pull away from us as they gravitate toward the other adult during this interaction. They put on masks that they never wear in normal life at home: the puppy dog eyes, the open-mouthed stare, and the sad pout. These are saved for special occasions when another adult is near.

In the span of just a few minutes, they are drawn farther and farther from us. They are pulled toward this other adult who is actually decreasing our own magnetism as their own magnetism increases. The pull is so strong that our magnetic child flips – the poles switch around, everything turns upside down, and we are no longer attractive, but repellant to our child.

We can't go with our child as he's being pulled away. We must stay in equilibrium, so he can find us later when he turns back around and this all shakes out.

And there will be shaking. Watch:

The other adult leaves. Bam! Like a flipped switch, the magnetic pull is cut off and gravity takes over, but unfortunately the parents are still repellant. Our child who has swung so far away starts to swing back, toward me, at me, past me, hot and cold, almost as far away now in the opposite direction. And back again. And back again. Ad nauseam.

The bond they started to feel toward the other adult is broken, though it never really existed in the first place. This confirms what they learned from their early years of institutional living, with the revolving door of caregivers who never stayed for long. The child is left with us, and they wonder, *How long is this really going to last? Someday, one of these new grown-ups will take care of me instead.*

He oscillates wildly for days or weeks until equilibrium is finally restored. The person who created the pull is long gone, smiling about the cute, charming child but a little unnerved with the uptight, controlling parents who just aren't who they used to be. This other adult is clueless about the havoc that took place after they left.

You don't have to see it to believe it. You will probably never see it.

> *It's so hard because their viewpoint is, "She went eight years without love and attention. Let's make up for that!" and I'm like,* **No**. *You have to* **stay away**.
>
> *I wish people really understood that we* **have** *to do things differently, and that those differences wouldn't weird them out or push them away. I also wish they understood that the "rules" aren't in place to alienate them or keep them away from my daughter — they are there to protect our new relationship together. What they could really do to help attachment would be to avoid interaction with her unless given permission. I wish I could put a sign on her that says "please do not hold me, touch me, or give me things." Lol.*
>
> *—adoptive mama*

Ha ha. No, seriously.

Here's why: There's a pizza party at school, and one of the students is a little girl with a severe allergy. Her parents provided a special lunch for her but the teacher feels bad about the girl missing out. *Surely the allergy isn't so serious she can't have just a small piece*, she thinks, and gives her some anyway. After class though, while the teacher is oblivious and the rest of the kids have gone home happy, that little girl is rushed to the emergency room.

It would be ridiculous, of course. There would be uproar and reprimands. There might be legal action. Most people are aware of severe allergies, diabetes, and other physical issues that cannot be fiddled around with. We don't have to understand all of the biological details in order to know that boundaries must be respected.

The same is true for attachment issues and other unseen special needs. If a parent says their child has special needs, **trust them and not just the child's appearance**[2] or your own experience. So much is at stake. There's no room for someone to disregard the boundaries simply because it seems unusual or mean.

In the next chapter we'll share a little about what the "emergency room" looks like with attachment issues. Lights sparkle, and sometimes there's even swearing in tongues. No exaggerating.

three

chaos in the sanctuary

It's bedtime, and a small boy approaches me with a large-eyed, questioning look.

"Kye fo my wam ba?" he asks. It sounds like some ancient tribal expletive.

His quick glance at the bathroom sink and uplifted water bottle translate the question for me. He's asking, "Can I fill my water bottle?" and he is actually able to say it perfectly. That's not the real question on his mind, though.

What he is *really* asking is, "How hard can I get you to work to understand what I'm saying? Can I control this situation? Can I control you?"

It's not a speech issue. It's an attachment issue. Many kids try to manipulate and control, but a child with a history of trauma and neglect actually thinks it is necessary for survival.

It's easier for him to control people that aren't familiar with his background, behavior, or needs.[1] He knows how to get their attention, how to manipulate their time, how to make them repeat themselves, and how to extort sympathy. It all feeds a craving for superficial attention so he can ignore his real need for genuine interaction with his mom and dad.

This craving is like a parasite living inside our children; they get very little of this superficial attention from their parents because it is not healthy for them. What they *do* get from their parents is a sanctuary of genuine connection from the same caregivers who are there for them day in and day out – which is a totally unfamiliar, scary, upside-down experience for many adopted children. They get honest love, guidance, and correction regarding behavior, hygiene, food, chores, school, manners, routines, everything. This depth of interaction is new and frightening, though it is healing for them.

Sons and daughters who arrive with a history of trauma often feel "bad," "dumb," and "unlovable." After all, they believe, "I was too bad for my birth family to keep. How can my adoptive parents and siblings love me?" They use their chronic behavioral challenges to validate this belief...

The child with a history of complex trauma has been dumped time and time again. Anger, to this son or daughter, creates distance in familial relationships. Anger inhibits attachment. Thus, the traumatized child thinks, "If I don't get too close, it won't hurt so much when you dump me." Behaviors—lying, stealing, peeing and pooping (in all the wrong places!), hoarding food,

mumbling, throwing homework out the bus window—
guarantee an argument and so, the adoptee believes,
"My heart is protected from further pain."

—Arleta James [2]

Adults do this sometimes, too. We push True Love away because we've been so burned by false idols that it's hard to trust the real thing when we see it. Sometimes the wounded create chaos to drive others away, especially when they don't want healing.

> *And He said to me, "Son of man, **do you see what they are doing**, the great abominations that the house of Israel are committing here, **to drive me far from my sanctuary?** But you will see still greater abominations."*
>
> *—Ezekiel 8:6*

The superficial attention-seeking beast tries to eat away at our children and their relationship with their family, fighting against the healing that they desperately need. As parents, we fight back with healthy, loving, genuine interaction. Additionally, we limit superficial interaction with others to starve the beast so the infection can heal and healthy tissue can regrow.

The beast has taught our kids some wily moves, though. Some of them are:

- False plays for sympathy (fake limping, postures, and body language that request sympathetic attention)
- Staring at someone to engage eye contact
- Animal or baby behavior/speech
- Purposefully slurred/garbled speech
- Feigned helplessness, or looking "lost"
- Going out of their way to walk in front of or between people to engage their attention

It feeds the beast when people reward these moves, and unfortunately, the visitor usually won't recognize the behaviors or be there later to endure the outcome. Playing his game results in other behaviors (or an increase of them) that the child and family have to deal with long after the visit is over, such as:

- lying
- sneaky behavior/stealing
- disobedience
- refusal to eat/wash/adhere to basic routines and self-care
- regression in potty training
- increase in tantrums/violence
- self-induced vomiting

My experience with bonding and attachment is that it often gets worse before it gets better. She is getting worse because kids who have not had that closeness with someone before are terrified of their strong feelings. We get strong feelings without getting terrified because we've had good experiences from others — intense closeness without getting abandoned or ignored. She is waging her own little war with her emotions.

—adoptive mother

This is the pendulum that swings when attention from other adults pulls them away from their parents. These children resist gravity until they learn they are safe in the sanctuary.

*Defiance is the big one that we see after someone has inappropriately crossed boundaries. Our kiddo will do things that outright defy rules and boundaries that he is familiar with in our home to see if we are going to hold to them. He also starts acting helpless or like a much younger child around **all** other adults after one adult "feeds the beast." We are forced to revert back to "tightening the reins" to how things were when the child first came home.*

*After the last time this happened, it was two weeks before we were able to get the child back to his normal. The backlash we experienced at home because one adult made the choice of "it's okay, I don't mind" (and can I just say that I hate that phrase every single time an adult says it, because it is **not** okay!) made me realize that even though this child has been home over three years and appears "fine" to those on the outside looking in, deep down, he is **not** "fine" and I can't ever forget that.*

—adoptive mom of four special needs children

They seem normal (whatever that is!) but their behavior with strangers is insincere – it is a mask covering a huge amount of anxiety. Creating chaos is a coping mechanism and they turn their world upside down as everything shakes out again. They simply don't know how to handle the attention they crave from others.

We wouldn't tell the parent of a diabetic child, "I feel so bad not giving candy to your child, it's so mean!" because we know that failing to respect the child's needs could send him or her to the hospital. In the same vein, adopted children do not need sympathy for boundaries set in place to bring about their healing. Sure, feel bad for the trauma, abandonment, neglect, and abuse they suffered that created the need for healing in the first place – their parents feel bad for that, too. Adoptive families feel grief over their child's past that outsiders can only imagine. But do not feel bad for the child over the measures their family must take to help them heal.

Expressing sympathy to them is not only pouring harmful bacteria into an already sick child, it is also insulting to their parents who are working so hard to facilitate their healing.

They are home. They are with a family. They *are* healing, being fed and loved, and no longer on the path to an asylum, a life of crime, or human trafficking.

Many of them, including our kids, are even learning English – and they can speak it with precision when they want to.

When the garbled gibberish at bedtime didn't get the reaction he was hoping for, my little guy decided to ask his question with perfect English, and just a slight accent.

"Sure," I answered. *Smile, mama.* "You can fill it right up to the number four" – I pointed to the four-ounce mark – "so you don't have an accident at bedtime." *Let's see how this goes.*

He said okay, and went to the bathroom sink. He came back with it filled to the –

No, wait. I won't tell you. Just guess. Pick a number, any number…ready?

It was the six ounce mark. And then (in perfect English) he said, "Is that good?" But what he's really asking is, *Can I make the rules, instead?*

And the answer is no. No way, Jose.

"No, dump it out, try again."

He sulked, refusing any water at all for a few minutes. Then he filled it to the five ounce mark, and tried the same song, second verse. "Is that good?"

Despite a strong, sudden urge to pour all five ounces on this adorable child, I did my best to muster a calm response: "Where did I say you could fill it to?"

He hesitated, then slowly pointed to the number...two. And yes, he knew what a four looks like. And no, I didn't dump the water on his head.

It's just that ridiculous sometimes. Keep laughing...we are all still learning here. Not perfect, desperate for grace, and clinging to Jesus and chocolate.

four

the heart of a mama,
the tangle with community

I don't know why I do this, but up until last month I was in the middle of making three different blankets — two quilts, one afghan — and then, with none of them even close to being finished, you know what I did?

Probably the same thing every crafter does before finishing three works in progress: I started another one.

I've made a few mistakes and unraveled the yarn to fix them, starting over. It's okay, though, because I've been doing this forever and have yet to meet a mistake — with yarn, at least — that can't be fixed. Stitch by stitch, it's a slow, steady process that calms me…nothing will happen with this yarn that I can't handle.

It's so comforting to have something we can plan, control, and fix, especially when there are so many things in life that are not so simple.

We stitch our families together in the face of various special needs, medical issues, personal circumstances, outside situations, and other distractions. There is a lot of unravelling that I have no idea how to fix. Our kiddos came unraveled, and my own ends fray often while trying to sort out the changes and adjustments.

After some thought, I think I can summarize my own challenges into three areas:

1. The children's behavior.

We've talked about that already. But because of that, or in the midst of that, there are two other major challenges. Get ready for a group hug, and grab a refill for your coffee:

2. My own heart as a mother.

This is where expectations collide with reality, and love conflicts with anger and frustration at being constantly repulsed (see #1) by these children who we want to love on and help heal. Faith constantly fights against fear.

We're learning to cope with the change in the culture of our home just as our adopted children are learning to live a new way of life. We walk the line between maintaining authority and dominion in the sanctuary while also modifying our lifestyle and routines in order to meet the needs of the broken.

Our own hearts change in the way we view parenting, motherhood, and family. The way we view joy. The way we view success. Everything is slow and small, one stitch at a time, and sometimes it unravels. We try not to feel like a failure because of how our children behave, because it's not about us and it's not even so much about them. It's about their broken past and their need to unlearn defective survival skills so they can learn to really live. It takes heaps of grace for us and them, picking up stitches and trying again.

We adjust our ideas of success. Progress is measured by greater lengths of time – not by days, but years. The healing is often two steps forward, one-point-nine steps back, and it's not always encouraging at the time…but after a year or so, we have a better vantage point and can see some real changes.

Oh, friends, remember the beginning? Those zombie-days of the first several months, when it felt like you were thrown into some awful never-ending reality show, in a strange, hostile environment with little chance of survival and dangerous creatures everywhere? Except the arena looked a little like your home, and the dangerous creatures sort of resembled your children?

It was the worst time in the world for the coffee pot to break down. And the washing machine. And the relationships. *And it was hard.* Many adoptive families say that their first year post-adoption was the hardest time in their lives, ever.

But then you stuck it out. You gave up on the coffee pot and switched to espresso (and friend, why didn't you do that years ago?). You learned a lot about tightening boundaries and fixing appliances. You hugged those who stayed close as your cocoon drew in tighter.

Our skin got thicker as our hearts got softer. And eventually, we could look across to…

…6 months later, when raging fits subsided from eight times a day to only, oh, maybe four times a day.

…12 months later, when a child used the toilet a little more consistently, no longer afraid of the scary Western potty, and poopy diapers from an eight-year-old (who swallows many things without chewing) finally became a rarity and *didn't even involve parasites* (yay!)…and yes, there were even days when raging fits were mostly gone.

…20 months later, when lying about obvious things ("Did you take Afton's marble?" "No." "Then how did it get in your pocket?") only happened a few times a week instead of several times a day.

…and we saw how far we've come. Not perfect, not as far as we wanted to be by now, but farther than we were.

It's like we started walking from a filthy dump and hoped to be a thousand miles away from the mess a year later – but after twelve months, we're only fifty miles away. It's kind of disappointing, and yet, it's progress. The smell is so much better than it was in the beginning. Some days still really stink, full of lying, defiance, and rages, but at least those days are diminished – usually – from what they used to be.

Once we have some things figured out (for the next five minutes, at least) with the moving target of behavioral issues and heart issues, there is another element that comes into play continually that can make or break us. Here is the third crucial challenge:

3. The assumptions, judgment, and/or apathy of the community at large.

And, oh, the unraveling. Why is this such a big deal?

> *Mostly it's people thinking they know better because the child behaves well in their presence and they contradict you about it in front of your child. Later, I pay dearly...*
>
> *...Our neighborhood doctor, dentists and teachers must be taught. We are in the winning stretch after the big race and professionals still can topple my family due to their choice of ignorance.*
>
> *—parent of child healing from Reactive Attachment Disorder*

For the most part, our culture has no clue about what is going on at a deeper level for adoptive families, and sadly, many people don't bother to find out before passing judgment, gossip, advice, etc. Adoptive parents often catch the scowling looks, and they hear the gossip, too (oh, yes we do!). Particularly among families working through attachment issues, there is one phrase we hear almost constantly when we set boundaries or try to explain some of the changes we put in place for our child's healing. It's like this, folks:

"Well, I think it's mean."

"But isn't that mean?"

"Oh, I couldn't ignore them, I'd feel so mean!"

And, well, that's easy to say when you're not the one dealing with an older child who is purposefully painting fecal matter on the walls, or trying to disentangle truths from lies out of that child's mouth dozens of times every day. It's not so easy to hear, though, when you're the parent in the trenches.

It's the "let them eat cake" of the attachment world.

You're so mean…you prob'ly think this chapter's about you…don't you? Don't you? It's not, though, friends, so please don't feel targeted…there's heaps of grace for all of us, on both sides, still learning. And we *thank you so much* for reading and being willing to learn alongside us.

The change in lifestyle, involvement, and enjoyment of church and community for adoptive families is a tricky balance. Even in the midst of worship with hands raised, eyes closed, and heart open, the sense of high-alert doesn't change – one of my hands is usually on Reagan's head or back the whole time so I can tell if the volume of the music or intensity of the environment starts to overwhelm her. I usually pat her instead of clapping to the music.[1]

We know that some people wonder why our adopted children sit with us in the service instead of going to the children's class. We tried it for months, but it was the wrong decision at the time – the same way we tried swimming lessons for bonding. The right treatment at the wrong time is still the wrong treatment, and we practice a lot of trial and error.

Every family has to learn what works best for their kids in the particular season they are in. Adoptive parents often get advice, suggestions, and opinions from people who don't even know where their kids are from.

And as a public service announcement on behalf of adoptive families, I want to share (in the sweetest, most loving tone possible) that simply because someone's brother, co-worker, friend, doctor, or plumber once adopted a child, it does not qualify that person to advise, counsel, or judge what adoptive families should do in any given situation, or how their child ought to be adjusting accordingly. Nor does a ten-minute Google search, a *Nightline* interview, reading *Pippi Longstocking* in the fourth grade, or watching any of the many wonderful film adaptations of *Jane Eyre* (not even the incredible one from 2006, my personal favorite).

I'm so sorry. More coffee, anyone?

Sometimes there's an awkward moment of brief explanation that probably leaves more questions than answers. Adoptive parents can't – and shouldn't – defend themselves by giving everyone all the gory details of their child's story and needs.

It would be mean for us to care more about the judgments of others and the comfort of our own social life than the progress and healing of our children. So, no. We're not mean. We're on high alert.

We miss events and often decline invitations. I walk on eggshells at every gathering and try to smile through it. We would love to let our guard down, but we've seen the consequences.

> *One thing I've observed and experienced on this journey is loneliness. Unloading on a friend is tough because, "Well (shrug), you signed up for this." That's like lecturing a friend on "signing up" for the side effects of chemotherapy. The path is tiresome, but worth it, and we still appreciate dear friends who bear the burden alongside us.*
>
> *—adoptive mom*

This upside-down life of trying to become a closely knit family when things often just feel like a tangled mess brings a new perspective for all of us – adoptive parents, adopted children, biological children, friends, family and community members. It's not perfect, but it's progress.

There are many stitches to go and we're not done yet, and He's not yet done with us, either. He gives us wisdom as we keep seeking, learning, trying, succeeding, failing, and trying again as He shows us how to tie up all of the loose ends...even the frayed ones.

five

what families wish for ...
besides coffee

We have discussed many times our inability to
respond to the statement, "I need help!" I have always
maintained this is not callousness, but inexperience.
It is not that we don't want to help, but that we don't
know how.

—Karen Burton Mains[1]

What do adoptive families wish for, other than healing? What do they need, besides respect and support over these hard boundaries, and buckets of coffee?

When a family has a baby, it's common to bring meals, offer help with older children, run errands, etc. We recognize this is a special time full of new memories: the new mama is recovering physically, everyone is exhausted, and no one is sleeping like they should. Laundry is piling up, and the cat is probably puking in all of the most inconvenient places.

And with adoption…guess what? It's very similar, except way harder.

Although the mama has not undergone childbirth, the entire family has just undergone a new heart-birth with the new child(ren) — and while the physical pain is not so severe, the emotional upheaval is often raw and intense. The family may be overcoming jetlag from living eleven hours out of their time zone for the last two weeks, and they might be completely unable to hold their eyes open past 5 pm during those first few days. It's possible that they hit the wall somewhere between the layover in Frankfurt and the customs desk at the homecoming airport.

Unlike a newborn who is easily contained (though loud and needy), adoptive parents are often caring for a child who is not an infant, not easily contained, and also loud and needy. Possibly, this child is also in diapers, but the mess is bigger and likely involves parasites. And with international adoption, they are unable to communicate their needs to their parents.

Delivered meals are a huge blessing. Gift cards. Grocery runs. May I also suggest...chocolate, coffee, and flowers?

There are many terrific articles out there on how to support newly adoptive families.[2] But what about later, after the jetlag has passed and some of the dust has settled?

I still suggest chocolate, coffee, and flowers. You really can't go wrong with those. Also, here's what other moms have to say:

I wish people would realize that asking questions about my daughter's birth family in front of her or making assumptions about her experience is not helpful or appropriate.

—adoptive mom

I wish people with no knowledge or experience with adoption would stop giving me unsolicited advice. I especially wish they would quit telling my adopted daughter things such as "You are a big girl and should not sit on your mother's lap." My child is unique, she has needs at all levels from infancy to teen...please give us support...not uninformed advice.

—adoptive mom

I wish that people understood the logistics that are involved with managing our daily life or in going to activities that other families take for granted. For example, this weekend we were invited to an impromptu pizza party. It was nice for them to invite us, and I think I might have hurt my friend's feelings when I declined. But something like that is incredibly hard for our family to manage even with both parents present...

We have one child with RAD who takes advantage of situations like that and will do everything he can to 1) break every possible rule, 2) hopefully triangulate a few adults and convince them that we are mean parents, 3) have a behavioral decline for 2-3 days after the event because of perceived injustices when 1 & 2 are thwarted. Another child is newly adopted, very cute and very engaging. We are constantly having to set up boundaries because he doesn't have any and he is like a beacon, pulling every single person in the room to come talk to him and kiss him and play with him. Of course they mean well, but that's not good for him right now. Tie all of that together and you can see why I declined. It was just too exhausting to even consider.

It would be amazing if people in our life realized how challenging an event like the above is for our family and volunteered in advance to help with some of the logistics. If the invitation had included "I'll help you with getting everyone fed" or "don't worry about getting to and from the car, we'll help" or "I know your son needs everyone to respect his need to attach, so I'll talk to everyone before you get here," then I would have been much more likely to accept.

—adoptive mom

Parents of children from hard places live with the judgment of others when we protect them, and we live with the consequences if we don't. Our kids experience further delays in healing, or regression from progress that we all clawed our fingernails bloody to get to in the first place.

Our children are older adoptees, and other families deal with so much more in both behavioral and health issues. Our children lived in institutions for years. Adoption begins with grief, and the child brings that grief into the family, and then everyone needs healing.

And the healing happens. It's happening here.

But it takes time. The "postpartum" healing with adoption takes much longer than four to six weeks.

Some of the biggest challenges personally have been:

1. Being perceived as the bad guy or the mean mom by family members, friends, and acquaintances (due to strict guidelines and boundaries).

2. Others not understanding the depth of the effects of trauma and loss in a child. One of our children was adopted as a toddler with no memories of life before us, but trauma's effects are still active six and a half years later. They don't just "get over it" in a few months after being home.

3. Social gatherings cause a great deal of stress and we have become pretty isolated. We have a laundry list of special needs that include sensory and hyperactivity and attachment... then there is the list of physical/medical needs that include cerebral palsy, blindness, incontinence, allergies, and more. Going out requires me to be on full alert as one child runs away and seeks strong sensory input, one child seeks affection from random adults, and yet another swirls in a downward spiral for days post-outing. Nobody seems to understand this. We have just been labeled hermits.

4. Finding a church we can be part of has been excruciating. We actually quit going for a few years. Nobody at church knew what to say to us. We did get a few [comments such as] "You have to be careful adopting someone else's kids with spiritual darkness attached to them," or something along those lines from a handful of people. When we were at the hospital for open-heart surgery we didn't have a single person from church or neighbors offer to help with our other children or bring a meal.

—adoptive mom

Delivered meals during hard seasons are a huge blessing for adoptive families, regardless of how long the child has lived with them. Our friends, family, and church encouraged us with their advocacy, kind words, boundaries, prayer, and gift cards. It wasn't flawless, but they learned alongside us and walked with us.

Six months after we brought Andrey and Reagan home, a dear couple from church called us after the service. Could they run by our house and drop something off really quick? Sure – and a few minutes later, the husband knocked on our door and surprised us with a small piece of paper. It was a four-figure check that covered the exact cost of our first two post-adoption reports.

A year after Andrey and Reagan came home, we went through a season of behavioral uproar and physical sickness involving eight loads of laundry a day and total emotional fatigue – and after a quick call on the cell phone to check in first, two of our closest friends came by with a latte, flowers, and hug. They might have brought something else, but I don't remember. I just remember how they stood on the porch with me while I cried and vented. They listened and understood, because they'd been there, too.

And recently I spent an hour on the phone with my sweet grandma. She's in her eighties and has been losing her vision, and some of her memory…and she asked questions again about the boundaries and the growth, the trauma and the healing, and the frustration and the progress. She asked the hardest questions in the gentlest manner. And she just listened again, and learned again, and loved me. Again.

We're all still learning, still walking.

> *I am so thankful for the people who understand this is challenging. We have a lot of people tell us our kids are just normal kids, but I really appreciate the ones who look at me quietly and say, "What you're doing is not easy, but you're doing a good job." Such simple words are like balm to my soul on the tough days.*
>
> *—adoptive mom*

SHANNON GUERRA

Moms, dads…listen closely. I'm going to listen, too. Ready?

What you are doing is not easy.

But you are doing a good job.

And it will be worth it.

conclusion

perspective that preserves us

Pussy willows grow wild here every spring, and I just love them. They only last a little while before they change and turn into leaves, all grown up.

When I was little my dad would cut small branches down and give them to me. Now my husband and oldest son collect them for me, and there's always a jar of pussy willows on our fireplace mantle or somewhere in the house. They don't need water, they're not fussy, they last forever. They're preserved right-side-up.

But other things need more care...like roses. Traditional roses don't grow wild here – they grow in the grocery store, seemingly right out of clear plastic bags. So convenient. My husband and sons occasionally, um, harvest those for me, too.

They don't last forever, though. To preserve them, we hang roses upside down so they hold their nutrients longer and keep their stems straight. Otherwise the flowers wilt, distorting the stem and shedding petals. Kept upright for too long, they collapse from the weight they carry.

If kept right side up, they fall to pieces.

> *The greatest among you shall be your servant.*
>
> *Whoever exalts himself will be humbled, and whoever humbles himself will be exalted.*
>
> *—Matthew 23:11-12*

Some of our kids are pussy willows – easily cared for, kept upright, not requiring anyone to bend over backwards to help them.

But some of our kids are more like roses. The world flips upside down in order to preserve them or they will collapse from the weight they carry. Their thorns must be handled with care.

> *But whoever would be great among you must be your servant, and whoever would be first among you must be your slave, even as the Son of Man came not to be served but to serve, and to give his life as a ransom for many.*
>
> *—Matthew 20:26b-28*

The view is different and our perspective changes. It has to, or we'll cause more damage to the child and isolate the family who is working so hard to help them heal.

If we really want what is best for a child, we must defer to the judgment of that child's parents regarding how, when, and if we can interact with the child healing from trauma and attachment issues.

> *When we are on the mom's side, we are on the child's side. When we take the child's side against the mom, they both lose.*
>
> —*Nancy Thomas[1]*

*When young girls are avoiding real love and looking for that acceptance in all the wrong places, we don't say, "It's okay to be a prostitute!" We say, "No, that's not real love!!" So why is it okay for our kids to "prostitute" themselves to teachers, church members, and other temporary caregivers so that the child will 'get their fill' without having to bond and experience **real love** and a permanent relationship with their parent? Well-meaning friends and acquaintances are telling our kids at four, six, ten, that it's okay to form temporary bonds, and they don't need their acceptance*

*and affection to come from the people that will be there
forever...**their parents**.*

—adoptive mom

*We still struggle with RAD, or I should say she does.
She has come so far, yet she still struggles at times. Pray
for God to show you [their] love language. These get
buried pretty deep, but I think they are the key. These
kids need to be whole in their relationships with us so
that they can be whole in their relationships with others.*

—adoptive mom of older daughter

We must rest assured that adoptive parents are more
concerned for the healing and welfare of their children
than anyone else is. They are in the trenches, rapidly
gaining boots-on-the-ground experience that no amount
of television talk shows or random internet perusal can
come close to. They are likely in frequent contact with
people experienced in trauma and attachment issues. Most
of the hours they used to have for free time are probably
now spent researching, praying, doing therapy, crying, and
going to appointments.

*An argument arose among them as to which of
them was the greatest. But Jesus, knowing the
reasoning of their hearts, took a child and put him*

by his side and said to them, "Whoever receives this child in my name receives me, and whoever receives me receives him who sent me. For he who is least among you all is the one who is great."

—*Luke 9:46-48*

Adoptive parents have more answers than the casual, curious observer, but…guess what? We have more questions, too.

We question ourselves more than anyone. It is harder on the family than it is on the guest when we ask them not to interact with children working through attachment issues. We feel worse than our guests do if the boundaries are crossed, because we are the ones who will be here to deal with the reversal of weeks of progress if one person thinks it's too "mean" to not give them friendly attention.

And he sat down and called the twelve. And he said to them, "If anyone would be first, he must be last of all and servant of all."

—*Mark 9:35*

We wonder how we can make things easier on everyone. We wonder if we'll ever have a normal social life again. We wonder if they can make coffee prescription-strength, because some days the over-the-counter variety just doesn't cut it.

Living upside down is messy – the new perspective is confusing, and sometimes we crash. We bleed when caught on the thorns of our little roses.

But He knows all about it. He wasn't just scratched by thorns; they were pressed into His head.

> *My friends, adoption is redemption. It's costly, exhausting, expensive, and outrageous. Buying back lives costs so much. When God set out to redeem us, it killed Him.*
>
> *—Derek Loux*

He models it for us. He always has. We follow Him, running toward all of our kids – the pussy willows, and the roses – just like He reaches for us. We all needed saving, adoption, and redemption at some point. We fall to pieces until we bend low for His perspective.

Despite our resistance, sin, hesitation, lack of trust, manipulation, control issues, fear...He loves us. In spite of all of it, He pursues us anyway. He is always running toward us.

further resources

- Families By Design (www.attachment.org) – articles and resources for parents, teachers, and therapists. Don't miss the article "Awesome Grandparenting for RAD"(not just for grandparents!): http://www.attachment.org/awesome-grandparenting-for-rad/ (accessed December 4, 2014).
- Attachment and Bonding Center of Ohio (www.abcofohio.net) – a ton of information, articles, services, and other resources.
- Empowered to Connect (www.empoweredtoconnect.org) – videos, articles, conferences, and other resources for attachment.
- Center for Cognitive-Developmental Assessment and Remediation (www.bgcenter.com) – Psychological services for internationally adopted children, including workshops, articles, education, and more. The article "Post Orphanage Behavior in Internationally Adopted Children" is a huge encouragement to international adoptive families (www.bgcenter.com/ BGPublications/ OrphanageBehavior.htm, Boris Gindis, April 2012, accessed December 4, 2014).

- Confessions of an Adoptive Parent (www. confessionsofanadoptiveparent.com) – Real-life wisdom and hope for families in the trenches.
- *Forever Mom* by Mary Ostyn (Thomas Nelson, 2014). Insight from a mama of ten children (four biological and six adopted) who has walked through the gamut of adoption – domestic and foreign, easy and hard, new baby and older child, siblings and special needs.
- *Get Your Joy Back* by Laurie Wallin (Kregel Publications, 2014). Wonderful resource for adoptive parents struggling with post-adoption depression, secondary trauma, and adjusting to life with special needs after adoption.

This is **a sample note** we have used for childcare providers. A variation of this personalized for your child and situation may be used for childcare workers, teachers, church staff, etc.

Andrey and Reagan both need detached professionalism and firm direction. No gushing or physical contact at all; any praise given needs to be specific and very matter of fact ("You did a great job coloring that blue," instead of a general "Great job!" or "You're a great kid!" type of compliment).

They should not have any one-on-one interaction with any adults that would signal that they are getting special treatment. If they try to seek out extra interaction, they should be directed to an activity (or toy) that they can enjoy without the help of an adult. Andrey is likely to volunteer over and over to help with things, and these offers should all be declined (because he is really attempting to control, not help).

The most important thing is to limit their direct interaction with adults as much as possible, and any necessary interaction must be brief and detached.

This is a **sample letter to a physician or medical provider**. It is crucial to find medical professionals who either understand attachment issues or are willing to learn about them. A variation of this personalized for your child and situation may be used and modified for that purpose.

Dear Dr. _____,

We want to touch base with you about our concerns with our son's attachment. We've been in contact with several people who are familiar with attachment issues in order to help him heal, bond, and resolve his attachment concerns. We appreciate the support you have shown for these adoptions and also the care you have given to all of our children.

We are learning that both Andrey and Reagan respond best to a very business-like, calm manner from people in the community. Any doting that happens to them from adults other than their parents will backfire in their attachment, and our family endures outbursts of increasingly negative, disruptive behavior for days afterward. We are helping them learn to be authentic in their interactions with others instead of triangulating with other adults, and if they are able to manipulate adults with superficial, "cute," or otherwise masking behavior, it reinforces that insincerity.

There are special challenges to dealing with attachment issues in a setting like a medical appointment. For example, we generally do not allow other adults to touch Andrey and Reagan because it is confusing for them in the bonding process, but they obviously must be touched by medical staff to have their vitals checked, blood drawn, etc. If this can be done in a very matter-of-fact, professional manner it does not always lead to behavioral fallout. The best-case scenario is that conversation and eye contact with Andrey and Reagan be limited as much as possible (they often seek out eye contact with strangers while avoiding eye contact with Vince and me) and that verbal encouragement or comfort comes from their parents only. We can also redirect the conversation through either of us to help this – for example, instead of asking Reagan or Andrey, "Step up on the scale," the staff can say, "He needs to step on the scale" to Vince or me, and we can direct them if necessary, though it is likely that they will comply just by overhearing.

Please let us know if you have any questions about any of this. It has taken us many months to discover this much about them, and every week brings new challenges and experiences to learn from. We appreciate your care for our family and for working with us to help Andrey and Reagan heal in body, mind, and spirit.

acknowledgments

Dozens of adoptive families contributed directly to this project. Some are quoted, many asked to remain anonymous, and all provided a vast spectrum of insight. Tremendous thanks to all of you who answered questions and shared your stories and comments – you gave me something to write about besides our own personal experience with attachment. And, friends…*what you are doing is not easy, but you are doing a good job.* I'm honored to walk this journey with you.

We have the deepest gratitude for our close friends and family who walked alongside us in humility and grace, willing and eager to learn about boundaries in attachment for our family's sake. Bacons, Bills, Dassows, and Thornsleys… you gave us safety in social gatherings and helped us avoid full-blown hermit status. You are all amazing, and we love you so much.

Cynthia Hellman, thank you so much for reviewing content and providing both editing and insight as an adoptive parent. Thank you also for checking in on me, encouraging me, making me laugh, and providing chocolate and prayer at crucial moments.

Joy Lynn McCavit, we are so thankful for you – for teaching us about attachment while we were still in the adoption process, for helping us through it after our kiddos came home, and for reviewing articles over the last year with encouragement and constructive feedback.

Many thanks to the dear readers who join me at Copperlight Wood as we listen for Jesus in the mundane and the mess.

Abundant love to my husband and kids, mighty champions of the cause. I love being in the battleship with each of you. This is a beautiful life, and you make it worth writing about.

Deepest gratitude to the Father, Son, and Spirit who bring meaning from the messes we make and victory to the clean-up operation. You are the Love Triumphant.

notes

introduction

1. For more information about the Home for Medical and Social Care for Children (HMSCC) Pleven orphanage and the improvements being made, please see the following links:

   Susanna Musser, "Will He Not Make It Good? Two Years in Pleven," *The Blessing of Verity*, www.theblessingofverity.com/2013/08/will-he-not-make-it-good-two-years-in-pleven (accessed August 30, 2013).

   The Pleven Project, "How It All Began," www.plevenproject.org/about.html (accessed November 5, 2014).

2. Please see Shannon Guerra, "Offering Chocolate: The Business of Redemption," *Copperlight Wood*, January 24, 2014, www.copperlightwood.com/2014/01/offering-chocolate-the-business-of-redemption.html.

one: the reality behind the rose-tinted movies

1. Please see *Parenting With Connection*, "The Inside Scoop: Fighters," www.parentingwithconnection. info/2014/02/the-inside-scoop-fighters, (accessed March 15, 2014).

two: the why behind the weird limits

1. Nancy Thomas, "Christmas Letter for Relatives of RAD," *Families By Design*, http://www.attachment.org (accessed March 31, 2014).

2. Please see Nancy Thomas, "Special Needs for Special Kids," *Families By Design*, http://www.attachment.org/ special-needs-for-special-kids (accessed March 31, 2014).

three: chaos in the sanctuary

1. Please see Kristin Berry, "Don't Save My Child," *Confessions of a Parent*, http://www.confessionsofaparent. com/dont-save-my-child (accessed March 31, 2014).

2. Arleta James, "Seeing the Forest Through the Trees: What to Pick?" *Attachment and Bonding Center of Ohio*, http://www.abcofohio.net/seeingforestthroughtrees. pdf (accessed March 31, 2014).

four: the heart of a mama, the tangle with community

1. Please see Shannon Guerra, "Conduit," *Copperlight Wood*, September 23, 2013, http://copperlightwood.com/2013/09/conduit.html.

five: what families wish for...besides coffee

1. Karen Burton Mains, *Open Heart, Open Home* (Elgin, Ill.: David C. Cook Publishing Co., 1976), 63-64.

2. These articles are full of information on how to help newly adoptive families:

   Julia DesCarpentrie, "How to Help an Adoptive Family," *MomLife Today*, http://momlifetoday.com/2011/11/how-to-help-an-adoptive-family (accessed March 20, 2014).

   Waiting to Belong, "Wrapping Around Adoptive Families," March 17, 2011, http://waitingtobelong.ca/articles/wrapping-around-adoptive-families-1 (accessed March 20, 2014).

conclusion: perspective that preserves us

1. Nancy Thomas, "RAD Child Emotional Heart Transplant," *Families by Design*, http://www.attachment.org/rad-child-emotional-heart-transplant (accessed March 1, 2013).

walk the line

some thoughts on boundaries, trust, and attachment

This is not just for the adoptive parent, or the prospective adoptive parent. This is not just for the person that comes into infrequent contact with adoptive parents or their children on the third Sunday, Tuesday, or Friday of every month.

It is for you. It is for me.

This addresses some of those questions from the fishbowl that no one wants to ask. Here is our heart-deep battle with the curtains drawn aside. Our home probably looks different from many others, though adoptive parents will probably find many similarities.

We're not perfect. We're learning. And we've noticed that the only people who are convinced they have it all figured out are those who have never adopted or had kids at all. Been there?

Grab your popcorn or coffee (or both) and enjoy.

Act One. The curtain rises. Six children, two cats, and one mama are in various stages of play, school work, and chores. Welcome to our living room.

We've had some extremely clean floors lately. They're just lovely. Our standard operating procedure around here is to assign extra chores to kids who need some extra discipline, and it's beautiful two-fold: in theory, the house gets a little cleaner; in practice, small hands are kept busy and (mostly) out of further trouble…for the time being, at least.

One of our favorite assigned chores is scrubbing the floor. The wonderful thing about this task is that most of our floor is made of large squares of faux tile that make this an easy assignment with clear boundaries to delineate.

I point to them and count them out as I walk the line: one, two, three, four. Turn left: uno, dos, tres. Multiplied, that's twelve easy squares. A child can see exactly where he's supposed to scrub. Simple…right?

Enter the child healing from attachment and control issues.

He scrubs half of the squares he is supposed to, and 93 others outside the lines. He's thinking, *"Will this work? Can I make the rules? What if I do this — it's not what you said, but sort of what you said, and I'm still doing my own thing? Can I be the boss? Because, look! I did extra!! Doesn't that count?"*

Nope. Negatory, dude.

Cue sound effects: sobbing and whining. It wavers for a second as he checks to see if I'm paying attention. This is a child headed for Broadway, already working on his first Tony.

Meanwhile in the next room, Reagan is standing on a chair where she was playing with the other kiddos a few minutes ago. She needs to get off the chair now, but she, too, is sobbing and whining, refusing to just...sit...down.

That's all.

She's squatting, her bottom only an inch from the seat. Without words, she is begging for someone to help her get down.

And no one helps. No one even offers.

> *It is so hard for people to understand because it doesn't make sense in the eyes of traditional parenting, but those of us parenting children who come to us via adoption are parenting children who have hurts that people can't see. If our children had a visible wound, then others could see it and would understand not to 'pick the scab' off, so to speak. Our kids have wounds that others can't see, so they don't know when they are picking the scab off.*
>
> *—adoptive parent*

We're not cruel; we're refusing to play. We know that she knows what to do: sit down, slide off the chair. We know that crooning over her or helping her do something that she is able to do herself will just throw gas on the fire – just because it's wet doesn't mean it will put the fire out.

What *is* cruel is that for almost seven years, it was easier and faster to do everything for her – brush her teeth, get her dressed, move her where she needed to go - and when we brought her out of the orphanage to the hotel when she was almost seven years old, she had no idea how to even sit in an adult-sized chair. Regular, non-baby toilets terrified her. She was an untrimmed plant that ran wild but spindly.

So we work all the time, every day, on small skills. Zipping. Snapping. Feeding herself without most of the food landing on the table, the clothes, or the floor. Using a real napkin to wipe her hands on at meals, instead of running sticky fingers through hair for the same purpose. During her first winter home, it took the entire season to teach her how to put on snowgear. But after seven months of snow, by spring she had achieved victory over snowpants, boots, and hat in less than 30 minutes.

She has learned so much and she knows what to do now in many situations. **The battle is deciding to obey, and then actually doing it.**

It's a universal struggle that, if we're honest, we adults are not immune to.

Another day, two more extra chores for the boy. I vaguely say "Scrub under and around the table," and he is fine – by my reckoning, he does about 25 squares worth. He's happy. He's done. Next chore please?

The next one is more specific: this area, and I point out the lines of an easy three-by-four rectangle, only twelve squares.

This is met with feigned panic and torture. Shocked sobbing at the injustice of it all. Whining and crying for ten minutes while scrubbing only part of the assigned area (and quite a bit extra). Ten minutes of constant wailing becomes almost like unheard white noise in the background until it's abruptly ended with a chipper, "Now can I be done?" that betrays the smoke and mirrors.

I check his chore. From the sheen of water on the ground I can clearly see that he scrubbed exactly two-thirds of the assigned area, and most of the rest of the room.

The boundaries are terrifying. Someone else is laying out rules and it is not him. He thinks he is seeing a cage, but what he is really facing is a fence to keep him from going over the cliff.

It's not limited to children from orphanages – some adults struggle with this, too. They started as children who never matured in the way of boundaries.

It's often revealed in the double-standard.

- *I don't have children and I know nothing about parenting, but you are really going to mess up your biological kids if you adopt.*

- *Let me preach to you about human rights while I advocate to have unborn children aborted if their existence is inconvenient. My pro-abortion bumper sticker is right next to the other one on the back of my Subaru that says "coexist."*

- *I can feel this way and be tolerant, but if you disagree with me, you are intolerant. I can say what I think because this is a free country, but if you say something I disagree with, I'll call it hate speech. And, by the way...you're the one that's judgmental and narrow-minded.*

Heads I win, tails you lose.

And I refuse to play. I won't croon, I won't cry, I won't enable, and I might not even argue. I've learned to draw a boundary and walk the line, and not let others cross it.

But I might laugh. We're getting lots of practice at this.

Act two. Manipulation and control issues manifest differently in children with a traumatic past.

The curtain rises on a new scene: Andrey is sitting in my lap waiting for a blood draw. His veins are iffy, and a nurse and a doctor are collaborating to find a good one. The needle hasn't touched him yet.

He starts to squirm and whimper, but I can tell from the position of his mouth that he is not afraid; he's masking for attention. It's an expression that took us a while to recognize — a cover that strangers take for gospel truth and adorable charm. This child wells up in crocodile tears when he sees two sympathetic, doting faces looking at him and crooning.

The crocodile tears are bait, though. He sells it, and they buy it - hook, line, and stinker. I mean, sinker.

I try to explain this to the professionals that are oohing and awwing and poor babying him. It's awkward because *he's right there* and I don't want to sound like a mean mama to him or to them. But I'm the one that will take him home after this, and they need to understand what's happening.

So I tell them. *This isn't genuine. Please just — no, it's not that — do you see this facial expression? He's not —*

Oh, it's okay, they say. They brush me off and pat his arm. They are searching for a vein, this arm, that arm, rubbing his arm, holding his hand, back to the other arm, maybe that one's better - and they continue smiling and fawning over him. He reads, *You poor baby. Your mommy just doesn't understand, does she?*

But they're playing the game, and it's really not okay. When they were finally done and looking the other direction, he smirked.

Fifteen minutes of overstimulation and poor boundaries led to more than a week of violent acting out, upheaval, and other misbehavior in our home. But it's okay. They weren't there for that.

Once the blood draw is finished, we go to the room where he gets to pick out a small treat from an overflowing box of made-in-China trinkets. I tell him to pick one out quickly because Dad and many siblings are in the tiny waiting room and we have more errands to run.

"Oh, it's okay – I told him he could have two," the doctor says.

Oh, perfect! Thank you so much for telling my son that the limits I set do not need to be enforced! Thank you so much for showing him that you are an authority over both of us. I'm sure you'll be happy to pay for anything that gets broken over the next three weeks, and also several therapy appointments? Those must be complimentary in your services, right? And you'll be there when it's not just his parents that set limits, but also when there are park rules, class expectations, and traffic laws…right? Right?

Hmm. Yeah…probably not.

And you know what? Without either of us noticing, he took three trinkets from the box. My husband found them as we were leaving.

He took more than he had permission from anyone to take, because *limits didn't matter.*

So it's not okay. If we are at the grocery store and I tell him he can only have one treat and he steals more, it's not okay. I'm grateful that we had the teaching opportunity over some cheap plastic toys and not over candy bars from the store, or worse.

I spoke to our doctor about it. We loved this office and their staff, and we knew that we were really on the same side. However, the week we lived through after that appointment was not acceptable and had to be addressed.

It was around the same time I had written an article about being on the same side, and the things God impressed on me then were still very fresh:

A gentle answer brings a gentle response.

*We confront successfully when we move from the mindset of someone being **in trouble** to being corrected **in love**.*

We're not perfect; we're all learning together. We're on the same side.

And I really tried. I tried to explain what our family went through the following week and how the boundaries Andrey needs to have in place are essential. I acknowledged that they were not treating him any differently than our other children, but explained that **he must be treated differently because his needs are different**.

You don't treat a child with a cancer the same way you treat a child with a cold.

I was met with a disturbing combination of condescension and defense, being blown off and berated. And we had to go back in a few months for another blood draw. Awesome.

We waited and researched. We made some phone calls and sent out emails to people who knew far more about attachment issues than we did, and they were not only a wealth of information, but also full of sympathy and encouragement. Anticipating our next appointment, we took what we gleaned from our resources and wrote a letter.

It was professional. It was kind. It was…educational. It was our line in the sand.

It was too much, apparently.

They said they wanted to be a warm, welcoming place for Andrey so he would feel safe and cared for.

Which is nice, except he needs to feel that from his family, not acquaintances and strangers. And he won't feel that from his family when the boundaries are pushed by other adults who are picking his scabs off. This makes him anything but safe. He would happily go home with any of their staff because they're still playing the game and putting gas on the fire. Helping him attach to the family he has is the issue we are concerned with, not his sense of hospitality in a medical office.

They said they didn't want to feel like they had to walk on eggshells every time our family came in for a visit. Our requests did not fit the bearings of their office and it would make the staff uncomfortable.

"Maybe our office just isn't the best fit for them," the doctor said. "I just really want what's best for Andrey and Reagan; they really deserve that."

I'm convinced that condescension is the ugliest form of pretense. It is a wounded ego oozing from an unteachable heart.

In our home, I told them, sometimes we walk on eggshells *all. day. long.* Not a day goes by that we are not walking the line.

But our odd little family with our odd little needs would cramp their style. It was time for some pruning.

So, adios. We walked the line right out of that pretty little office and straight into a new one, and our special needs didn't cramp *their* style at all.

It's okay. We can still root for each other. We can be on the same side without being on the same team. Some of us are clearly playing entirely different sports.

Act 3. The curtain rises. It is months later.

It is a hard day, and I'm holding a fighting boy who is mad at the world.

He's mad at his choices, mad at his consequences, and especially mad at his mama for walking the line with him.

I look into dark eyes and tell him not to fight me because **I am on his side**, and when he fights me, he fights against himself...and he is the one that loses.

> *RAD is so bizarre, and parenting them is so backward in many ways. It really is an experience where you learn about God's love for us though, because it is often years of loving them with no love in return. If other adults give them attention, it only makes it worse and prevents them from attaching to the parents longer. So many parents, though, feel so judged as they try to parent these kids.*

In order to parent them effectively you have to quit caring about what others may think and care only about what is best for the child. [That's] hard to do as a first time RAD parent and I think why so many disrupt. Hard enough to have your child not love you, but then to have others judging you, too, is just too much for many. I try to remind people that if the child is "reacting" then it is because they are "attaching" even if you aren't seeing it and feeling it. If they didn't feel themselves wanting to get close to you then there wouldn't be so many behaviors.

—adoptive mom

We make it to lunchtime.

It's a treat for most of us on this day because we have veggie sushi. I know Andrey and Reagan don't like it, though, and there's just enough cucumber in the fridge to make an alternate meal for them – *tarator*, a traditional Bulgarian cold soup that they love. I don't usually accommodate with options, but we need to use the ingredients up anyway and it sounds good to me. Perfect.

I'm grating cucumber. "I don't like sushi," Andrey announces from the table, amid cheers from the other kids who love it.

"I know. I'm making tarator for you and me and Reagan."

I finish grating the cucumber and start chopping mint leaves (not sure if these are traditional, but I like them).

"I don't like soup. I want sushi," he says. I mix in yogurt, drizzle in olive oil.

"I want sushi," he repeats.

Sprinkle salt and pepper. I'm getting tired of these announcements and make one of my own.

"Today I'm not going to feed you food that you complain about. If you complain about something, you will not get it, whether you change your mind or not."

Silence. I can hear him coming to a realization. The wheels are turning.

I arrange seven dishes. Sushi for four kids, tarator for Reagan and myself. Bread and apples for everyone.

Lots of bread and apples for Andrey. And he says nothing, but his mind is learning. Those wheels are still turning, and he's trying to decide if he wants to steer down the straight and narrow, or try driving through the fence.

Someone asks for tea, and I start pouring.

"I don't like tea," he announces.

"That's okay, you have a water bottle."

A few minutes pass. We have prayed and we are eating. We are happy…six of us, at least.

"May I pwease have tea?" he asks aloud. But what he is really asking is, *Did you mean what you said when you said I couldn't have something I complain about? Or can I get you to let me get away with pushing the rules?*

Can I set a moving target?

And the answer is no. No, no, and no. "You have a water bottle," I remind him. *Remember to smile, mama.*

"I don't wike my water bottle." And then he gets a look on his face that clearly says, *Oh, crap.*

And he is learning what I want to teach him, instead of the other way around. We have set a boundary and he is learning to respect it. To respect others. To respect himself.

We knew there was progress. There had to be. But it didn't feel like it when we hit our one-year anniversary and both kiddos seemed to be regressing in one form or another.

We knew that what we were doing must be working to some degree because they were rejecting it. Sincerity pushes them out of their comfort zone, and a year into this, suddenly basic routines were out the window and met with defiance.

Not asking to be excused at meals. Not asking to have a chore checked. Not flushing the toilet (*so help me*) without being reminded.

It's a game that's not fun for anyone. The reminder isn't necessary.

Patience is.

Also, liquor.

Just kidding.

The lunch scene replays itself a couple of weeks later, shortly after our one year anniversary. Sushi for some of the kids, *tarator* for others.

"Oh! Yummy sushi! I wike sushi! I wike soup, too!"

Well, you don't say.

We don't want to over-prune, and neither can we under-prune. We must prune with a purpose, looking forward to a thriving life that will bear much fruit.

It's hard to walk the line every day. We're not heroes. We continue to covet your prayers…and your occasional gifts of coffee and chocolate.

May adoptive and foster families find encouragement, healing, and grace as they walk the line throughout their community, in all of their days. The victory is here.

End of Act 3. Curtain closes.

Do you want more encouragement, more
camaraderie, more real life – unpolished, imperfect,
but finding peace in the hard moments and
beauty in the mess? A place where we learn to
see the sacred in the midst of the mundane?

You are warmly invited to copperlightwood.com, to rest,
refuel, and renew your purpose for the season you are in.

White space in the chaos. Holiness in the hardship.
And sentence fragments, sometimes.

His peace is for you,

Shannon Guerra

email: shannon@copperlightwood.com
subscribe: eepurl.com/MugpP
facebook.com/copperlightwood
instagram.com/copperlightwood